# New Generative AI SaaS Startup

## Startup

Unlock the Power of AI to Transform Your Startup

By Hugh Webb

I0011975

Copyright 2023 All rights reserved. No part of this book may be reproduced or transmitted in any form or by any means, electronic or mechanical, including photocopying, recording or by any information storage and retrieval system, without permission in writing from the publisher.

# Disclaimer:

The information contained in this book is for general informational purposes only. The author and publisher make no representations or warranties of any kind, express or implied, about the completeness, accuracy, reliability, suitability or availability with respect to the book or the information, products, services, or related graphics contained in the book for any purpose. Any reliance you place on such information is therefore strictly at your own risk.

In no event will the author or publisher be liable for any loss or damage including without limitation, indirect or consequential loss or damage, or any loss or damage whatsoever arising from loss of data or profits arising out of, or in connection with, the use of this book.

The information and techniques contained in this book are not intended to diagnose, treat, cure, or prevent any medical or psychological condition. If you have any health concerns or conditions, it is strongly advised that you consult with a qualified healthcare provider before starting any new stress management techniques or lifestyle changes. The information and advice in this book is not a substitute for professional medical or psychological treatment.

This book is intended for informational and educational purposes only, and it is not intended as a substitute for professional advice, diagnosis, or treatment. Always seek the advice of your physician, mental health professional, or other qualified health provider with any questions you may have regarding a medical or psychological condition.

# Table of Contents

# The Purpose of This Book

The purpose of this book is to provide a comprehensive guide for entrepreneurs, investors, and industry professionals interested in generative AI SaaS startups. By exploring topics such as defining generative AI SaaS, understanding the target market, creating a business plan, developing a pricing strategy, and preparing for acquisition or IPO, this book provides a roadmap for success in this exciting and rapidly evolving industry. In addition, this book will provide insights into emerging trends and opportunities, as well as potential ethical and data privacy concerns associated with generative AI. Overall, the goal of this book is to equip readers with the knowledge and tools necessary to start and grow a successful generative AI SaaS startup, while also promoting responsible and ethical business practices in this emerging field.

# Chapter 1: Definition of Generative AI SaaS

Artificial Intelligence (AI) has rapidly transformed the way we live, work, and communicate. The advent of Machine Learning (ML) and Deep Learning (DL) techniques has enabled the development of sophisticated AI models that can perform complex tasks and generate new content. One such area of AI is Generative AI, which has the potential to create new, unique content with the help of AI models.

Generative AI refers to the use of AI algorithms to create original content such as images, music, text, and videos. Unlike traditional AI models that are trained to recognize and classify existing data, generative AI models generate entirely new data that did not exist before. This is made possible by leveraging advanced neural networks and other machine learning techniques that allow the AI system to learn from large datasets and generate outputs that mimic human creativity.

Software as a Service (SaaS) refers to a software delivery model where software is made available to users over the internet, typically on a subscription basis. SaaS has become increasingly popular in recent years because it allows businesses to access advanced software applications without having to worry about the underlying hardware and software infrastructure.

Generative AI SaaS combines the power of generative AI with the flexibility of SaaS delivery model. It enables businesses to access sophisticated AI models that can generate new content and insights, without the need to invest in expensive hardware or software infrastructure. Instead, businesses can subscribe to a generative AI SaaS platform and access the AI models through a web interface or API.

Generative AI SaaS can be used in a variety of applications such as content creation, advertising, design, and even scientific research. For example, a content creation company can use a generative AI SaaS platform to generate unique images or videos for their clients. An advertising agency can use it to generate copy for their campaigns, and a designer can use it to generate new ideas and concepts for their projects.

In summary, Generative AI SaaS is a powerful combination of AI and SaaS delivery model, enabling businesses to access sophisticated AI models that can generate new content and insights. As the demand for AI-powered solutions continues to grow, Generative AI SaaS is poised to become an increasingly important part of the AI landscape.

Chapter 2: Why Generative AI SaaS is Important

The rise of generative AI SaaS has the potential to transform the way businesses operate, allowing them to automate tasks, increase efficiency, and create unique content. Here are some of the key reasons why generative AI SaaS is important:

Improved Efficiency and Productivity: Generative AI SaaS can help businesses automate tasks and processes, which in turn increases efficiency and productivity. For example, a content creation company can use generative AI SaaS to automatically generate new images or videos for their clients, freeing up staff time for more complex tasks.

Creation of Unique Content: Generative AI SaaS can generate new and unique content that can be used in a variety of applications such as advertising, design, and scientific research. This content can help businesses stand out from their competitors and provide a competitive advantage.

Scalability: Generative AI SaaS can scale to meet the needs of businesses of all sizes, from small startups to large enterprises. This allows businesses to access advanced AI models without having to invest in expensive hardware and software infrastructure.

Cost-Effective: Generative AI SaaS is cost-effective compared to building and maintaining in-house AI infrastructure. Businesses can pay for what they need, when they need it, without having to worry about the underlying technology infrastructure.

Access to Advanced Technology: Generative AI SaaS provides businesses with access to advanced AI models that they might not have the resources to develop in-house. This can help businesses stay competitive in a rapidly changing business landscape.

Innovation: Generative AI SaaS can help businesses innovate and create new products and services that were not previously possible. By leveraging the power of generative AI, businesses can create new content and insights that can drive innovation and growth.

Ethical Considerations: With the rise of AI-powered solutions, ethical considerations have become increasingly important. Generative AI SaaS can help businesses ensure that their AI models are developed and used in an ethical and responsible manner, by providing tools for transparency, explainability, and bias mitigation.

In summary, generative AI SaaS is important because it can help businesses improve efficiency, create unique content, scale, reduce costs, access advanced technology, drive innovation, and ensure ethical considerations. As businesses continue to adopt AI-powered solutions, the importance of generative AI SaaS is only set to increase.

# Chapter 3: Current State of the Generative AI SaaS Market

The market for generative AI SaaS is rapidly growing, with many companies and startups developing and offering innovative solutions. Here are some of the key trends and insights into the current state of the generative AI SaaS market:

1. Market Size: The generative AI market is expected to grow at a CAGR of 41.5% from 2020 to 2027, with a total market size of $1.5 billion by 2027.
2. Adoption Rate: The adoption rate of generative AI SaaS is increasing, as businesses look to automate tasks, increase efficiency, and create unique content. According to a recent report, 66% of organizations are planning to implement some form of AI technology, including generative AI, in the near future.
3. Verticals: Generative AI SaaS is being adopted across a wide range of verticals, including advertising, design, content creation, music, and scientific research.
4. Competitive Landscape: The generative AI SaaS market is highly competitive, with many established players and startups offering innovative solutions. Some of the leading companies in the market include OpenAI, IBM, and Google.
5. Use Cases: Generative AI SaaS is being used for a variety of use cases, such as image and video creation, music composition, and text generation. It is also being used to develop advanced AI models for scientific research and analysis.
6. Challenges: The generative AI SaaS market faces several challenges, including ethical considerations, data privacy, and explainability. As AI models become more complex, it becomes increasingly important to ensure that they are developed and used in an ethical and responsible manner.

7. Opportunities: The generative AI SaaS market offers many opportunities for startups and established companies to develop innovative solutions and capture market share. As the market continues to grow, there is a huge potential for companies to develop new use cases and applications for generative AI.

In summary, the generative AI SaaS market is rapidly growing, with increasing adoption rates across a wide range of verticals. While the market faces several challenges, such as ethical considerations and data privacy, it offers many opportunities for startups and established companies to develop innovative solutions and capture market share. As the demand for AI-powered solutions continues to grow, the generative AI SaaS market is set to become an increasingly important part of the AI landscape.

# Chapter 4: Major Players in the Generative AI SaaS Industry

The generative AI SaaS market is highly competitive, with many established players and startups offering innovative solutions. Here are some of the major players in the industry:

1. OpenAI: OpenAI is a non-profit AI research company that develops advanced AI models for a wide range of applications. They offer a range of generative AI SaaS solutions, including GPT-3, a language generation platform, and DALL-E, an image generation platform.
2. IBM: IBM is a multinational technology company that offers a range of AI solutions, including generative AI SaaS. Their Watson platform offers solutions for natural language processing, image and video analysis, and music composition.
3. Google: Google is a leading technology company that offers a range of AI-powered solutions, including generative AI SaaS. Their Magenta platform offers solutions for music and art creation, and their Cloud AI platform offers solutions for natural language processing, image and video analysis, and more.
4. Adobe: Adobe is a software company that offers a range of creative solutions, including generative AI SaaS. Their Adobe Sensei platform offers solutions for image and video creation, natural language processing, and more.
5. Nvidia: Nvidia is a leading technology company that offers a range of AI-powered solutions, including generative AI SaaS. Their NVIDIA Jarvis platform offers solutions for natural language processing and speech recognition, and their NVIDIA Omniverse platform offers solutions for 3D content creation.

6. Microsoft: Microsoft is a multinational technology company that offers a range of AI-powered solutions, including generative AI SaaS. Their Azure AI platform offers solutions for natural language processing, image and video analysis, and more.
7. Hugging Face: Hugging Face is a startup that offers a range of generative AI SaaS solutions, including GPT-2 and GPT-3 models for natural language processing, and DALL-E models for image generation.

In summary, the generative AI SaaS industry is highly competitive, with many established players and startups offering innovative solutions. OpenAI, IBM, Google, Adobe, Nvidia, Microsoft, and Hugging Face are some of the major players in the industry. As the demand for AI-powered solutions continues to grow, it is likely that we will see more players entering the market and more innovative solutions being developed.

Chapter 5: Emerging Trends and Opportunities in the Generative AI SaaS Industry

The generative AI SaaS industry is constantly evolving, with new trends and opportunities emerging all the time. Here are some of the emerging trends and opportunities in the industry:

1. Niche solutions: With the market becoming more crowded, there is an opportunity for companies to develop niche solutions that cater to specific use cases or verticals. For example, startups are emerging that offer generative AI solutions for fashion design, interior design, and other industries.

2. Human-AI collaboration: As AI models become more advanced, there is a growing trend towards human-AI collaboration. This involves using generative AI to augment human creativity and productivity, rather than replace it entirely. For example, generative AI can be used to generate ideas, designs, or music that humans can then refine and improve.

3. Explainable AI: As AI models become more complex, there is a growing need for explainable AI. This involves developing AI models that can explain their decision-making process in a way that humans can understand. This is particularly important for generative AI, where the output can be unpredictable and difficult to interpret.

4. AI ethics: There is a growing awareness of the ethical implications of AI, particularly in the context of generative AI. As AI models become more advanced, there is a risk that they may perpetuate biases or create content that is harmful or offensive. As a result, there is an opportunity for companies to develop ethical guidelines and best practices for generative AI.

5. User-generated content: User-generated content is becoming increasingly popular, and there is an opportunity for generative AI to play a role in its creation. For example, generative AI could be used to generate personalized music, art, or video content based on user preferences.
6. Low-code solutions: There is a growing trend towards low-code and no-code solutions, which allow non-technical users to create complex applications without the need for coding. There is an opportunity for generative AI to be integrated into these platforms, making it easier for users to create content and applications.

In summary, the generative AI SaaS industry is constantly evolving, with new trends and opportunities emerging all the time. Niche solutions, human-AI collaboration, explainable AI, AI ethics, user-generated content, and low-code solutions are just some of the emerging trends and opportunities in the industry. As the industry continues to grow and mature, we can expect to see more innovative solutions and use cases for generative AI.

Chapter 6: Identifying a Problem to Solve with Generative AI SaaS

If you're thinking of starting a generative AI SaaS startup, the first step is to identify a problem that your solution can solve. Here are some steps to help you identify a problem to solve with generative AI SaaS:

1. Identify an industry or market: The first step is to identify an industry or market that could benefit from generative AI. Some industries that are currently using or could benefit from generative AI include fashion, music, art, interior design, and advertising.

2. Identify pain points: Once you've identified an industry or market, the next step is to identify pain points or challenges that could be addressed with generative AI. For example, in the fashion industry, designers may struggle to come up with new and innovative designs. In the music industry, artists may struggle to come up with new melodies or chord progressions.

3. Research existing solutions: Before developing your solution, it's important to research existing solutions in the market. This will help you to understand what's currently available and identify any gaps that your solution could fill.

4. Define your solution: Once you've identified a pain point, the next step is to define your solution. This could involve developing a generative AI model that addresses the pain point, or building a platform that allows users to generate content using AI.

5. Validate your solution: Before launching your solution, it's important to validate it with potential customers. This could involve conducting surveys or focus groups to gather feedback on your solution, or offering a beta version of your product to early adopters.

6. Refine your solution: Based on the feedback you receive, you may need to refine your solution to better address the pain points of your target market. This could involve tweaking the algorithms used in your generative AI model or adding new features to your platform.

In summary, identifying a problem to solve with generative AI SaaS involves identifying an industry or market, identifying pain points, researching existing solutions, defining your solution, validating your solution, and refining your solution based on feedback. By following these steps, you can develop a solution that addresses a real need in the market and has the potential to be successful.

# Chapter 7: Understanding the Target Market for Your Generative AI SaaS Startup

To build a successful generative AI SaaS startup, it's important to have a deep understanding of your target market. Here are some steps to help you understand your target market:

1. Define your ideal customer: The first step is to define your ideal customer. This could involve creating a customer persona, which outlines the characteristics and needs of your ideal customer. This will help you to tailor your solution to their specific needs.

2. Identify the pain points of your target market: Once you've defined your ideal customer, the next step is to identify the pain points and challenges that they face. This could involve conducting market research, surveys, or interviews with potential customers.

3. Research your competition: To understand your target market, it's important to research your competition. This will help you to understand what solutions are currently available and how you can differentiate your solution from others in the market.

4. Understand the buying process: It's important to understand the buying process of your target market. This could involve understanding the decision-making process of your target customers, as well as their budget and purchasing criteria.

5. Develop a pricing strategy: Based on your understanding of the market and the competition, you can develop a pricing strategy that is competitive and reflects the value of your solution.

6. Develop a marketing strategy: Once you have a deep understanding of your target market, you can develop a marketing strategy that effectively targets your ideal customer. This could involve social media marketing, content marketing, or other channels that are popular among your target market.

7.  Gather feedback: It's important to continually gather feedback from your target market to ensure that your solution is meeting their needs. This could involve conducting surveys or focus groups, as well as monitoring user behaviour and engagement with your solution.

In summary, understanding the target market for your generative AI SaaS startup involves defining your ideal customer, identifying pain points, researching your competition, understanding the buying process, developing a pricing and marketing strategy, and gathering feedback. By following these steps, you can build a solution that effectively addresses the needs of your target market and has the potential to be successful.

Chapter 8: Building a Team for Your Generative AI SaaS Startup

To build a successful generative AI SaaS startup, it's important to have a strong and diverse team in place. Here are some steps to help you build a team:

1. Define roles and responsibilities: The first step is to define the roles and responsibilities that you'll need on your team. This could involve hiring a data scientist, software engineers, UX/UI designers, marketing and sales personnel, and project managers, among others.

2. Hire for diversity: To build a strong team, it's important to hire for diversity. This could involve hiring people with different backgrounds, experiences, and perspectives. This will help to foster creativity and innovation within your team.

3. Look for relevant experience: When hiring for your team, it's important to look for relevant experience. This could involve hiring people who have experience with generative AI, machine learning, software development, or other related fields.

4. Hire for culture fit: In addition to hiring for skills and experience, it's important to hire people who will fit well with your company culture. This will help to ensure that your team works well together and is aligned with your company's mission and values.

5. Offer competitive compensation and benefits: To attract top talent, it's important to offer competitive compensation and benefits. This could involve offering competitive salaries, equity, health insurance, and other perks.

6. Provide ongoing training and development: To help your team stay up to date with the latest developments in generative AI and related fields, it's important to provide ongoing training and development opportunities.

7. Foster a collaborative and inclusive culture: To build a strong and effective team, it's important to foster a collaborative and inclusive culture. This could involve holding team-building activities, encouraging open communication, and providing opportunities for feedback and recognition.

In summary, building a team for your generative AI SaaS startup involves defining roles and responsibilities, hiring for diversity, looking for relevant experience, hiring for culture fit, offering competitive compensation and benefits, providing ongoing training and development, and fostering a collaborative and inclusive culture. By following these steps, you can build a team that is capable of building and scaling a successful generative AI SaaS solution.

# Chapter 9: Creating a Business Plan for Your Generative AI SaaS Startup

To build a successful generative AI SaaS startup, it's important to have a well-defined business plan in place. Here are some steps to help you create a business plan:

1.  Define your mission and vision: The first step is to define your company's mission and vision. This could involve outlining the problem you're solving, your target market, and your long-term goals.
2.  Conduct market research: To create an effective business plan, it's important to conduct market research. This could involve analyzing the market size and growth potential, identifying your competitors and their strengths and weaknesses, and understanding your target customer's needs.
3.  Define your solution: Based on your market research, define your generative AI SaaS solution. This could involve outlining its features, benefits, and how it solves your target customer's pain points.
4.  Create a go-to-market strategy: Once you've defined your solution, create a go-to-market strategy. This could involve outlining your sales and marketing tactics, pricing strategy, and distribution channels.
5.  Develop a financial plan: To ensure the sustainability of your business, it's important to develop a financial plan. This could involve outlining your revenue streams, expenses, and projected profitability.
6.  Define your team and resources: Based on your business plan, define the team and resources you'll need to build and scale your generative AI SaaS solution. This could involve outlining the skills and experience you'll need, as well as the technology and infrastructure required.

7. Create a timeline and milestones: Finally, create a timeline and milestones for your business plan. This will help you to track your progress and make adjustments as needed.

In summary, creating a business plan for your generative AI SaaS startup involves defining your mission and vision, conducting market research, defining your solution, creating a go-to-market strategy, developing a financial plan, defining your team and resources, and creating a timeline and milestones. By following these steps, you can create a well-defined business plan that will help you to build and scale a successful generative AI SaaS solution.

# Chapter 10: Funding Options for Your Generative AI SaaS Startup

To build and scale your generative AI SaaS startup, you'll need to secure funding. Here are some of the funding options you can consider:

1. Bootstrapping: Bootstrapping involves funding your startup with your own personal funds or revenue generated by your business. This can be a good option for startups that are just getting started and have yet to generate revenue.
2. Friends and family: Another option is to seek funding from friends and family members. This can be a good option if you have a network of people who believe in your vision and are willing to invest in your startup.
3. Angel investors: Angel investors are wealthy individuals who invest their own personal funds in startups. They typically invest at an early stage and provide funding in exchange for equity in the company.
4. Venture capital: Venture capital firms provide funding to startups in exchange for equity in the company. They typically invest in startups that have a high growth potential and a strong team.
5. Crowdfunding: Crowdfunding involves raising funds from a large group of people, typically through online platforms. This can be a good option if you have a strong online presence and a compelling story.
6. Grants: There are a variety of grants available for startups in the technology sector. These can be a good option if you meet the eligibility requirements and can secure funding without giving up equity in your company.

7.  Accelerators and incubators: Accelerators and incubators provide funding and support to startups in exchange for equity in the company. They typically provide mentorship, networking opportunities, and other resources to help startups grow and scale.

When considering funding options for your generative AI SaaS startup, it's important to weigh the pros and cons of each option. Some options may require giving up equity in your company, while others may require repayment or interest payments. By understanding the different options and their requirements, you can make an informed decision that will help you to secure the funding you need to build and scale your generative AI SaaS solution.

In summary, funding options for your generative AI SaaS startup include bootstrapping, seeking funding from friends and family, seeking investment from angel investors and venture capital firms, crowdfunding, applying for grants, and participating in accelerators and incubators. By considering these options and weighing the pros and cons of each, you can secure the funding you need to build and scale your generative AI SaaS solution.

# Chapter 11: Developing the Product Roadmap for Your Generative AI SaaS Startup

A product roadmap is a high-level plan that outlines the product vision and the steps needed to achieve it. Developing a product roadmap is an essential part of building a successful generative AI SaaS startup. Here are the steps to developing your product roadmap:

1. Define your product vision: Your product vision should articulate the problem you are solving and the value you are providing to customers. This should be clear and concise and serve as a guidepost for the rest of your product development.

2. Conduct market research: Market research is essential to understanding your target audience and their needs. This can help you identify gaps in the market and develop features and functionalities that will appeal to your customers.

3. Prioritize features: Once you have a list of potential features, you'll need to prioritize them. This involves evaluating the impact and effort of each feature and determining which ones are most critical to the success of your product.

4. Create a timeline: With your features prioritized, you can create a timeline that outlines when each feature will be developed and released. This can be broken down into shorter-term sprints that align with your development cycles.

5. Communicate the roadmap: Once you have developed your product roadmap, it's important to communicate it with your team and stakeholders. This ensures everyone is aligned and working towards the same goals.

6. Iterate and adjust: As you develop your product and receive feedback from customers, you may need to adjust your roadmap. This requires a willingness to iterate and adjust your plan as needed.

By following these steps, you can develop a product roadmap that outlines your product vision, identifies key features and functionalities, and provides a timeline for development and release. This roadmap can serve as a guidepost for your development team and ensure that everyone is aligned and working towards the same goals.

In summary, developing a product roadmap is an essential part of building a successful generative AI SaaS startup. It involves defining your product vision, conducting market research, prioritizing features, creating a timeline, communicating the roadmap, and iterating and adjusting as needed. By following these steps, you can create a roadmap that outlines your product vision and provides a clear path to achieving it.

Chapter 12: Choosing the Right AI Technology for Your Generative AI SaaS Startup

Choosing the right AI technology is critical for the success of your generative AI SaaS startup. Here are some important considerations when choosing the right AI technology for your product:

1. Purpose: The first step in choosing the right AI technology is to identify the purpose of your product. This will help you narrow down the type of AI technology that is best suited for your needs.
2. Data requirements: The quality and quantity of data required for your AI technology is another important consideration. The type of data and how it is collected can have a significant impact on the performance of your AI technology.
3. Algorithm selection: There are many different AI algorithms to choose from, and the selection will depend on the purpose of your product and the type of data you are working with. Some common algorithms include neural networks, decision trees, and support vector machines.
4. Model training: Once you have selected your algorithm, you will need to train your model. This involves using your data to optimize the performance of your algorithm.
5. Integration: The integration of your AI technology with your SaaS platform is another important consideration. The integration should be seamless and easy to use, without disrupting the user experience.
6. Scalability: The ability to scale your AI technology is also important. You need to ensure that your AI technology can handle an increasing amount of data as your user base grows.

7. Cost: Finally, cost is an important consideration when choosing AI technology. The cost of AI technology can vary significantly depending on the algorithm, data requirements, and level of customization.

By considering these factors, you can choose the AI technology that is best suited for your generative AI SaaS startup. This will help you develop a product that is effective, scalable, and affordable. It will also help you stay competitive in the market and meet the needs of your target audience.

In summary, choosing the right AI technology is critical for the success of your generative AI SaaS startup. This requires considering the purpose of your product, data requirements, algorithm selection, model training, integration, scalability, and cost. By carefully evaluating these factors, you can choose the AI technology that is best suited for your needs and develop a product that is effective, scalable, and affordable.

Chapter 13: Designing the User Interface for Your Generative AI SaaS Startup

Designing the user interface (UI) for your generative AI SaaS startup is a critical aspect of the product development process. A well-designed UI can help users understand the functionality of your product, enhance user experience, and promote adoption. Here are some key considerations when designing the UI for your product:

1.  User-Centered Design: Your UI should be designed with your target users in mind. This means understanding their needs, preferences, and expectations. Conduct user research, gather feedback, and analyze user behavior to develop a UI that is tailored to your users' needs.
2.  Simplicity: Your UI should be simple and intuitive. Avoid overwhelming your users with too much information or too many features. Use clear and concise language and avoid complex jargon.
3.  Consistency: Consistency in design is important for creating a familiar and predictable user experience. Use consistent visual elements, typography, and color schemes to reinforce your brand and enhance the user experience.
4.  Accessibility: Ensure that your UI is accessible to all users, including those with disabilities. Consider using accessibility guidelines and standards such as WCAG 2.1 to make your product usable by as many people as possible.
5.  Visual Hierarchy: Use visual hierarchy to guide users through the UI and highlight important information. This can be achieved through the use of font sizes, colors, and placement.

6. Feedback and Confirmation: Provide clear feedback to users when they interact with your UI. Use confirmation dialogs to confirm actions that can't be undone.
7. Responsive Design: Your UI should be designed to be responsive across different devices, including desktops, tablets, and mobile devices. Use responsive design techniques to ensure that your UI is accessible and functional on any device.

In summary, designing the UI for your generative AI SaaS startup requires careful consideration of your users' needs, simplicity, consistency, accessibility, visual hierarchy, feedback, and confirmation, and responsive design. By focusing on these elements, you can develop a UI that enhances the user experience, promotes adoption, and drives the success of your product.

Chapter 14: Ensuring Scalability and Performance for Your Generative AI SaaS Startup

Scalability and performance are critical considerations when building a generative AI SaaS startup. As your user base grows and your product becomes more complex, you need to ensure that your system can handle the increased load and maintain high performance. Here are some key considerations when designing and building a scalable and performant system:

1. System Architecture: Your system architecture should be designed to handle increased loads and traffic. Consider using microservices or a serverless architecture to enable scalable and flexible computing.

2. Load Testing: Perform load testing to simulate high traffic and identify any bottlenecks or performance issues. Load testing can help you optimize your system performance and identify areas that need improvement.

3. Caching: Use caching to reduce the load on your system and improve performance. Caching can be used to store frequently accessed data in memory or on disk, reducing the need for repeated queries.

4. Data Management: Ensure that your data management practices are optimized for performance and scalability. Use techniques such as sharding, replication, and indexing to manage and access data efficiently.

5. Cloud Infrastructure: Consider using cloud infrastructure to provide scalable and cost-effective computing resources. Cloud providers such as AWS, Azure, and Google Cloud provide a range of services for scaling and managing your system.

6. Automation: Automate processes such as deployment, monitoring, and scaling to improve efficiency and reduce the risk of errors. Automation can help you respond to changes in traffic and usage in real-time.

7. Monitoring and Analytics: Monitor your system performance and usage to identify issues and optimize performance. Use analytics tools to gain insight into user behavior and system performance.

In summary, ensuring scalability and performance is essential for the success of your generative AI SaaS startup. By designing a scalable and performant system architecture, load testing your system, using caching, optimizing data management practices, using cloud infrastructure, automating processes, and monitoring and analyzing performance, you can build a system that can handle high traffic and usage, and provide a great user experience for your customers.

# Chapter 15: Identifying the Right Marketing Channels for Your Generative AI SaaS Startup

Marketing is a critical component of building a successful generative AI SaaS startup. To ensure that your product reaches the right audience, you need to identify the most effective marketing channels for your target market. Here are some key considerations when choosing the right marketing channels for your generative AI SaaS startup:

1. Identify Your Target Audience: To identify the right marketing channels, you need to understand your target audience. Who are they? What are their pain points? Where do they go for information? By understanding your target audience, you can tailor your marketing strategy to reach them effectively.

2. Consider Your Budget: Different marketing channels have different costs associated with them. Consider your budget when choosing marketing channels. Are you willing to invest in paid advertising or do you prefer to focus on organic growth?

3. Utilize Social Media: Social media is a powerful tool for reaching your target audience. Identify the social media platforms your target audience uses most frequently and create a social media strategy to engage with them.

4. Leverage Content Marketing: Content marketing is a great way to demonstrate your expertise in the field and build brand awareness. Consider creating blog posts, whitepapers, videos, or webinars to educate and engage your target audience.

5. Attend Industry Conferences and Events: Attending industry conferences and events is a great way to network with potential customers and partners. Identify the conferences and events that your target audience is likely to attend and create a plan to engage with attendees.

6. Use Email Marketing: Email marketing is an effective way to stay in touch with your customers and leads. Consider creating a newsletter or email campaign to keep your target audience up-to-date on your product and company news.
7. Invest in SEO: Search engine optimization (SEO) is critical for driving organic traffic to your website. Optimize your website for relevant keywords and ensure that your content is high-quality and useful for your target audience.

In summary, identifying the right marketing channels is essential for the success of your generative AI SaaS startup. By understanding your target audience, considering your budget, utilizing social media, leveraging content marketing, attending industry conferences and events, using email marketing, and investing in SEO, you can build a comprehensive marketing strategy that reaches your target audience effectively and drives growth for your business.

Chapter 16: Developing a Pricing Strategy for Your Generative AI SaaS Startup

Developing a pricing strategy for your generative AI SaaS startup is critical to the success of your business. Your pricing strategy will impact how much revenue your company generates, how your product is perceived in the market, and how you compare to your competitors. Here are some key considerations when developing a pricing strategy for your generative AI SaaS startup:

1. Understand Your Costs: Before you can set your pricing, you need to understand your costs. Calculate your fixed and variable costs, and determine your break-even point. This information will help you set a minimum price for your product.

2. Consider Your Value Proposition: What is the value that your generative AI SaaS product provides to customers? Are you solving a critical business problem or providing a unique value proposition that no other product on the market can match? Your pricing should reflect the value that your product provides.

3. Research Your Competitors: Understand how your competitors price their products and what features they offer at different price points. You may want to price your product similarly or use your pricing to differentiate your product from competitors.

4. Choose a Pricing Model: There are several pricing models to consider, including per-user pricing, per-feature pricing, usage-based pricing, and value-based pricing. Consider which model makes the most sense for your product and target audience.

5. Test Your Pricing: Conduct pricing experiments to determine what price point resonates with your target audience. A/B test different price points and measure the impact on customer acquisition and revenue.

6. Consider Bundling and Discounts: Consider bundling your product with other products or services to increase the perceived value of your offering. Offer discounts for long-term commitments or large purchases to incentivize customers to choose your product over competitors.

7. Stay Flexible: Your pricing strategy should not be set in stone. As your business grows and evolves, you may need to adjust your pricing strategy to ensure that it continues to meet the needs of your customers and your business.

In summary, developing a pricing strategy for your generative AI SaaS startup is a critical step in building a successful business. By understanding your costs, considering your value proposition, researching your competitors, choosing a pricing model, testing your pricing, considering bundling and discounts, and staying flexible, you can create a pricing strategy that maximizes revenue, satisfies customers, and positions your product for success in the market.

# Chapter 17: Sales Tactics for Your Generative AI SaaS Startup

Sales tactics are critical to the success of your generative AI SaaS startup. Even the best product will not sell itself without an effective sales strategy. Here are some key considerations when developing your sales tactics:

1. Develop a Sales Process: A well-defined sales process helps ensure that your sales team is consistent and efficient in their sales efforts. Your sales process should outline the steps that your sales team takes to move a potential customer from initial contact to a closed sale.

2. Define Your Ideal Customer Profile: Your ideal customer profile should include demographics, company size, industry, pain points, and other criteria that make a customer a good fit for your product. This information will help your sales team target the right prospects and ensure that they are spending their time and resources on the most promising leads.

3. Train Your Sales Team: Your sales team needs to be equipped with the right skills, knowledge, and resources to effectively sell your product. Provide your sales team with product training, sales training, and resources such as case studies, sales collateral, and competitive intelligence.

4. Leverage Referral Marketing: Referral marketing is a powerful way to generate leads and close sales. Encourage satisfied customers to refer others to your product by offering incentives, such as discounts or free services.

5. Offer Trials and Demos: Trials and demos allow potential customers to experience your product first-hand, which can be a powerful selling tool. Consider offering free trials or demos to qualified prospects.

6. Create Compelling Sales Collateral: Your sales collateral, including your website, pitch deck, and other marketing materials, should be visually appealing, concise, and compelling. It should clearly articulate your value proposition and address potential objections.
7. Follow Up and Nurture Leads: Following up with leads is critical to moving them through your sales funnel. Develop a follow-up process that includes personalized communications, such as phone calls or emails, to nurture leads and keep them engaged.
8. Monitor and Optimize Your Sales Efforts: Regularly review your sales metrics, such as conversion rates, lead sources, and deal size, and use this data to optimize your sales efforts. Continuously refine your sales process, messaging, and tactics to improve your results.

In summary, effective sales tactics are critical to the success of your generative AI SaaS startup. By developing a sales process, defining your ideal customer profile, training your sales team, leveraging referral marketing, offering trials and demos, creating compelling sales collateral, following up and nurturing leads, and monitoring and optimizing your sales efforts, you can build a successful sales strategy that generates revenue and drives growth for your business.

# Chapter 18: Establishing Customer Relationships for Your Generative AI SaaS Startup

Establishing and maintaining strong customer relationships is crucial to the success of your generative AI SaaS startup. Here are some key considerations when building and maintaining customer relationships:

1. Deliver Exceptional Customer Service: Your customers expect exceptional service, and it is up to your team to deliver it. Be responsive, helpful, and empathetic when dealing with customer inquiries and issues. Make sure your customers know they are valued and that you are committed to their success.

2. Provide Regular Product Updates and Enhancements: Your product should be designed to evolve with your customer's needs. Regular updates and enhancements demonstrate that you are listening to customer feedback and are committed to continuously improving your product.

3. Solicit Customer Feedback: Regularly ask your customers for feedback to understand their needs, pain points, and how you can improve your product. This feedback can inform your product development and improve customer satisfaction.

4. Establish Customer Success Programs: Your customer success team should work with customers to ensure they are getting the most out of your product. Establish a formal customer success program that includes regular check-ins, personalized training, and other resources to help customers achieve their goals.

5. Personalize Your Communications: Personalized communication, such as personalized emails and customer-centric messaging, can help establish a stronger relationship with your customers. Make sure your communications are tailored to the customer's needs and pain points.

6. Build a Community: Build a community of your customers where they can share ideas, experiences, and feedback. This community can also serve as a valuable resource for your product development team.
7. Offer Loyalty and Referral Programs: Offering loyalty and referral programs can help incentivize customers to continue using and referring your product. Consider offering discounts or free services for repeat customers or for customers who refer others to your product.
8. Continuously Measure and Optimize Customer Satisfaction: Regularly measure customer satisfaction metrics, such as Net Promoter Score (NPS), and use this data to optimize your customer relationships. Continuously refine your customer success programs, personalized communications, and loyalty and referral programs to improve customer satisfaction and retention.

In summary, establishing strong customer relationships is critical to the success of your generative AI SaaS startup. By delivering exceptional customer service, providing regular product updates and enhancements, soliciting customer feedback, establishing customer success programs, personalizing your communications, building a community, offering loyalty and referral programs, and continuously measuring and optimizing customer satisfaction, you can build long-term relationships with your customers and drive business growth.

# Chapter 19: Expanding the Product Offering for Your Generative AI SaaS Startup

Expanding the product offering of your generative AI SaaS startup is an important step in ensuring long-term growth and success. Here are some key considerations when expanding your product offering:

1. Understand Your Customers' Needs: Before expanding your product offering, it is essential to understand your customers' needs and pain points. Talk to your customers, gather feedback, and conduct market research to identify areas where your product can be expanded to better meet their needs.

2. Identify Complementary Products or Services: Look for products or services that complement your existing product and that your customers may also need. These complementary products or services can help you expand your customer base and revenue streams.

3. Develop a Roadmap: Develop a roadmap for expanding your product offering, including timelines, resources needed, and key milestones. This roadmap should align with your overall business strategy and be regularly updated as new information becomes available.

4. Leverage Existing Technology: Leveraging existing technology can help you expand your product offering more efficiently and effectively. For example, if you have developed a generative AI technology that is used in your current product, you may be able to apply it to new products or services.

5. Consider Partnerships and Acquisitions: Partnerships and acquisitions can help you quickly expand your product offering and enter new markets. Consider partnering with other companies or acquiring companies with complementary products or services.

6. Test and Iterate: Before launching new products or services, it is important to test and iterate to ensure that they meet your customers' needs and expectations. This can involve conducting user testing, running pilot programs, and gathering feedback from beta customers.

7. Communicate Changes to Customers: When expanding your product offering, it is important to communicate changes to your customers. This can include providing product demonstrations, offering free trials, and hosting webinars or other events to showcase your new offerings.

In summary, expanding your product offering is a crucial step in ensuring the long-term growth and success of your generative AI SaaS startup. By understanding your customers' needs, identifying complementary products or services, developing a roadmap, leveraging existing technology, considering partnerships and acquisitions, testing and iterating, and communicating changes to customers, you can successfully expand your product offering and continue to drive business growth.

# Chapter 20: Scaling the Team for Your Generative AI SaaS Startup

As your generative AI SaaS startup grows and expands, it will become necessary to scale your team to support the increased workload and new business opportunities. Here are some key considerations when scaling your team:

1. Understand Your Team's Capabilities: Before hiring new team members, it is important to understand your existing team's capabilities and identify any gaps that need to be filled. This can involve conducting skills assessments and performance evaluations to identify areas for improvement.

2. Define Roles and Responsibilities: Clearly define roles and responsibilities for new team members to ensure that everyone understands their responsibilities and is working towards the same goals. This can involve developing job descriptions and organizational charts that outline the reporting structure and responsibilities of each team member.

3. Hire the Right People: When hiring new team members, it is important to find the right people who have the skills, experience, and values that align with your company's culture and goals. This can involve conducting thorough interviews, checking references, and conducting background checks to ensure that you are hiring the best candidates.

4. Provide Adequate Training and Support: Once new team members are hired, it is important to provide adequate training and support to ensure that they are able to perform their jobs effectively. This can involve providing onboarding programs, mentorship opportunities, and ongoing training and development programs.

5. Foster Collaboration and Communication: Foster a culture of collaboration and communication among your team members to ensure that everyone is working towards the same goals and sharing information and knowledge. This can involve hosting regular team meetings, setting up communication channels, and creating a supportive and inclusive work environment.
6. Manage Resources Effectively: As your team grows, it is important to manage resources effectively to ensure that everyone has the tools and resources they need to perform their jobs effectively. This can involve investing in technology and infrastructure, as well as managing budgets and resources.
7. Monitor Performance and Adjust as Needed: Regularly monitor team performance and adjust as needed to ensure that everyone is meeting expectations and working towards the company's goals. This can involve conducting performance evaluations, setting clear goals and objectives, and providing ongoing feedback and coaching.

In summary, scaling your team is an essential part of growing and expanding your generative AI SaaS startup. By understanding your team's capabilities, defining roles and responsibilities, hiring the right people, providing adequate training and support, fostering collaboration and communication, managing resources effectively, and monitoring performance and adjusting as needed, you can successfully scale your team and continue to drive business growth.

# Chapter 21: Creating a Sustainable Business Model for Your Generative AI SaaS Startup

Creating a sustainable business model is essential for the long-term success of your generative AI SaaS startup. Here are some key considerations when creating a sustainable business model:

1. Define Your Value Proposition: Define your unique value proposition and how it aligns with the needs of your target market. This involves identifying the key benefits of your generative AI SaaS solution and how it solves the problems of your target customers.

2. Identify Your Revenue Streams: Identify your revenue streams and how they will be generated. This can involve subscription-based pricing, usage-based pricing, or other revenue models that align with your target market and the benefits of your generative AI SaaS solution.

3. Determine Your Cost Structure: Determine your cost structure and how it will impact your pricing and revenue streams. This can involve identifying the key expenses associated with developing, marketing, and selling your generative AI SaaS solution, as well as ongoing expenses such as infrastructure, maintenance, and customer support.

4. Establish a Competitive Advantage: Establish a competitive advantage that sets your generative AI SaaS solution apart from other solutions on the market. This can involve identifying your unique value proposition, building a strong brand, and creating a loyal customer base.

5. Focus on Customer Acquisition and Retention: Focus on customer acquisition and retention to ensure that your generative AI SaaS solution is able to generate sustainable revenue over time. This involves identifying the key channels and tactics for acquiring new customers, as well as strategies for retaining and upselling existing customers.
6. Invest in Research and Development: Invest in research and development to continue improving your generative AI SaaS solution and staying ahead of the competition. This can involve allocating resources towards developing new features, improving performance, and staying up to date with emerging trends and technologies.
7. Manage Risks and Uncertainties: Manage risks and uncertainties associated with the generative AI SaaS industry to ensure that your business is able to weather any potential challenges or disruptions. This involves identifying potential risks and developing contingency plans to mitigate their impact on your business.

In summary, creating a sustainable business model is essential for the long-term success of your generative AI SaaS startup. By defining your value proposition, identifying your revenue streams and cost structure, establishing a competitive advantage, focusing on customer acquisition and retention, investing in research and development, and managing risks and uncertainties, you can create a sustainable business model that drives long-term growth and profitability.

# Chapter 22: Preparing for Acquisition or IPO for Your Generative AI SaaS Startup

As your generative AI SaaS startup grows and becomes more successful, you may consider the possibility of acquisition or going public with an initial public offering (IPO). Here are some key considerations when preparing for acquisition or IPO:

1.  Build a Strong Financial Foundation: Ensure that your generative AI SaaS startup has a strong financial foundation with clear revenue streams and a sustainable business model. This involves generating positive cash flow, demonstrating revenue growth, and establishing a solid financial track record.

2.  Establish a Strong Brand and Market Presence: Establish a strong brand and market presence that sets your generative AI SaaS solution apart from the competition. This can involve building a strong customer base, establishing a loyal following, and developing a reputation for quality and innovation.

3.  Develop a Talented and Experienced Team: Develop a talented and experienced team that can drive growth and innovation within your generative AI SaaS startup. This involves hiring top talent, retaining key employees, and developing a culture of excellence and collaboration.

4.  Develop Strong Partnerships and Alliances: Develop strong partnerships and alliances with other businesses in the generative AI SaaS industry that can help to drive growth and innovation. This can involve collaborating with other companies to develop new products or services, sharing resources and expertise, and leveraging industry knowledge and insights.

5. Comply with Regulations and Standards: Comply with all relevant regulations and standards in the generative AI SaaS industry to ensure that your business is operating in a legal and ethical manner. This involves staying up to date with evolving regulatory requirements and ensuring that your business is in full compliance with all relevant laws and standards.

6. Engage in M&A or IPO Readiness Activities: Engage in mergers and acquisitions (M&A) or IPO readiness activities to prepare your generative AI SaaS startup for a successful acquisition or IPO. This can involve conducting due diligence, preparing financial statements and projections, and developing a comprehensive business plan that demonstrates the potential for growth and profitability.

7. Seek Expert Guidance and Support: Seek expert guidance and support from experienced professionals in the M&A or IPO space to ensure that your generative AI SaaS startup is well positioned for success. This can involve working with investment bankers, attorneys, and other professionals with experience in the acquisition or IPO process.

In summary, preparing for acquisition or IPO requires building a strong financial foundation, establishing a strong brand and market presence, developing a talented and experienced team, developing strong partnerships and alliances, complying with regulations and standards, engaging in M&A or IPO readiness activities, and seeking expert guidance and support. By following these key considerations, you can position your generative AI SaaS startup for a successful acquisition or IPO and drive long-term growth and profitability.

Chapter 23: Data Privacy and Security Concerns for Your Generative AI SaaS Startup

As a generative AI SaaS startup, it's crucial to prioritize data privacy and security to protect your customers' sensitive information and maintain their trust. Here are some key considerations when it comes to data privacy and security:

1. Protect Data with Strong Encryption: Ensure that all data is protected with strong encryption and that encryption keys are stored securely. This can help to prevent unauthorized access to data, mitigate the risk of data breaches, and comply with data protection regulations.

2. Implement Access Controls: Implement access controls to ensure that only authorized personnel can access sensitive data. This can involve using multi-factor authentication, role-based access controls, and other security measures to prevent unauthorized access.

3. Conduct Regular Security Audits: Conduct regular security audits to identify potential vulnerabilities and areas for improvement. This can involve conducting regular penetration testing, vulnerability assessments, and code reviews to identify potential security risks.

4. Comply with Data Protection Regulations: Comply with all relevant data protection regulations, such as the General Data Protection Regulation (GDPR) and the California Consumer Privacy Act (CCPA). This involves understanding the specific requirements of each regulation, implementing appropriate measures to protect data, and appointing a data protection officer to oversee compliance.

5. Provide Transparency and Control: Provide transparency and control over how customer data is collected, used, and shared. This can involve providing customers with clear and concise privacy policies, obtaining explicit consent for data collection and use, and offering customers control over their data.
6. Train Employees on Data Privacy and Security: Train all employees on data privacy and security best practices to ensure that they understand the importance of protecting sensitive data and know how to identify and report potential security threats.
7. Respond to Data Breaches Promptly: Have a plan in place to respond to data breaches promptly, including notifying affected customers and regulatory bodies as required. This can help to minimize the impact of data breaches and maintain customer trust.

In summary, prioritizing data privacy and security is essential for any generative AI SaaS startup. This involves protecting data with strong encryption, implementing access controls, conducting regular security audits, complying with data protection regulations, providing transparency and control over customer data, training employees on data privacy and security, and responding to data breaches promptly. By following these key considerations, you can protect customer data and maintain their trust, which is critical to the success of your generative AI SaaS startup.

# Chapter 24: Ethical Considerations for Your Generative AI SaaS Startup

As a generative AI SaaS startup, it's essential to consider the ethical implications of the products you're developing and the impact they may have on society. Here are some key ethical considerations to keep in mind:

1. Bias and Fairness: AI models are only as unbiased as the data they're trained on. This means that if your data is biased, your AI will be too. It's important to ensure that your data is representative and diverse to avoid perpetuating existing biases in society. Additionally, consider implementing fairness metrics and approaches to ensure that your AI doesn't discriminate against certain groups.

2. Privacy: Respect your customers' privacy by being transparent about the data you collect, how it's used, and who has access to it. It's essential to obtain explicit consent from customers before collecting their data and to only use it for the specific purposes outlined in your privacy policy.

3. Responsibility: As the creators of an AI model, you have a responsibility to ensure that it's being used in a responsible manner. Consider implementing ethical guidelines for the use of your product and monitor its usage to ensure it's not being used in ways that are harmful or unethical.

4. Explainability: It's important to ensure that your AI model is explainable and transparent, so users can understand why a certain decision was made. This is especially important when it comes to making decisions that may impact people's lives, such as in healthcare or hiring.

5. Safety: Ensure that your AI model is safe and won't cause harm to users or society. Consider conducting risk assessments and implementing safety measures to prevent unintended consequences.
6. Human Oversight: While AI can automate many tasks, it's important to have human oversight to ensure that it's being used in a responsible and ethical manner. Additionally, consider involving diverse stakeholders in the development and testing of your AI to ensure that it's serving the needs of society as a whole.

In summary, ethical considerations are essential for any generative AI SaaS startup. This involves considering bias and fairness, privacy, responsibility, explainability, safety, and human oversight. By following these ethical principles, you can ensure that your AI is being used in a responsible and ethical manner, which is critical to the success of your generative AI SaaS startup.

## Chapter 25: Competing with Established Players in the Generative AI SaaS Industry

As a new entrant in the generative AI SaaS industry, competing with established players can be challenging. However, there are several strategies you can employ to help your startup gain a foothold in the market:

1. Focus on a Niche: Identify a specific market segment that isn't being served by the established players and create a product that addresses their unique needs. By focusing on a niche, you can differentiate your product from the offerings of the established players and build a loyal customer base.

2. Offer a Better User Experience: User experience is critical for SaaS products, and offering a better user experience than the established players can be a significant competitive advantage. Invest in creating a user-friendly interface and intuitive features that make it easy for customers to use your product.

3. Offer Better Pricing: One advantage of being a new entrant is the ability to offer better pricing than the established players. Consider offering more affordable pricing plans or a pricing model that is more flexible than what the established players offer.

4. Partner with Established Players: Partnering with established players can help your startup gain access to a larger customer base and increase brand awareness. Consider partnering with established players who offer complementary products or services to yours.

5. Innovate: Innovation is key to staying competitive in the SaaS industry. Keep up with the latest trends in generative AI and continually update your product to stay ahead of the competition. Consider investing in R&D to develop new features or functionalities that set your product apart from the offerings of the established players.

6. Build a Strong Brand: Building a strong brand is critical for success in the SaaS industry. Establish your brand as a thought leader in the generative AI space by producing thought-provoking content, engaging with your customers on social media, and participating in industry events.

In summary, competing with established players in the generative AI SaaS industry requires a strategic approach. Focusing on a niche, offering a better user experience, providing better pricing, partnering with established players, innovating, and building a strong brand are all strategies that can help your startup gain a foothold in the market. By implementing these strategies, you can successfully compete with established players and establish your startup as a leader in the generative AI SaaS industry.

Chapter 26: Staying Ahead of the Curve in the Generative AI SaaS Industry

In the rapidly evolving world of generative AI SaaS, staying ahead of the curve is critical for success. To maintain a competitive advantage and ensure long-term success, it's essential to keep up with the latest trends and innovations in the industry. Here are some strategies to help you stay ahead of the curve:

1. Stay Up-to-Date with the Latest Technologies: As a generative AI SaaS startup, you must stay up-to-date with the latest technologies and trends in the industry. Attend industry events, read industry publications, and participate in online forums to keep yourself informed of the latest developments in the field.

2. Foster a Culture of Innovation: Foster a culture of innovation within your company to encourage your team to think creatively and experiment with new ideas. Encourage your team to attend conferences, workshops, and other industry events to learn about the latest trends and technologies in the field.

3. Leverage Data Analytics: Use data analytics to monitor customer behavior and identify trends and patterns. Analyze user feedback and usage metrics to identify areas for improvement and develop new features that meet the needs of your customers.

4. Engage with the Community: Engage with the generative AI community to stay informed of the latest developments in the field. Participate in online forums and social media groups to connect with other professionals and share insights and ideas.

5. Build Strategic Partnerships: Build strategic partnerships with other companies in the industry to stay abreast of the latest trends and innovations. Collaborate with other companies to develop new products or services that address emerging market needs.
6. Invest in R&D: Invest in research and development to develop new features and functionalities that differentiate your product from those of your competitors. Conduct market research to identify emerging market trends and develop new features that meet the evolving needs of your customers.

In summary, staying ahead of the curve in the generative AI SaaS industry requires a commitment to ongoing learning and innovation. By staying up-to-date with the latest technologies, fostering a culture of innovation, leveraging data analytics, engaging with the community, building strategic partnerships, and investing in R&D, you can maintain a competitive advantage and ensure long-term success in the industry.

Chapter 27: Recap of Key Points in Building a New Generative AI SaaS Startup

Starting a new generative AI SaaS startup is a complex and challenging process that requires careful planning and execution. In this book, we covered a wide range of topics related to building a successful generative AI SaaS startup. Here is a recap of some of the key points covered in this book:

1. Definition of Generative AI SaaS: Generative AI SaaS refers to a cloud-based software service that uses machine learning algorithms to generate creative and novel content, such as images, music, or text.

2. Importance of Generative AI SaaS: Generative AI SaaS can provide users with a range of creative content that is tailored to their specific needs, resulting in greater engagement and satisfaction.

3. Current State of the Market: The generative AI SaaS market is still relatively new, but it is growing rapidly, with new players entering the market every day.

4. Major Players in the Industry: Some of the major players in the generative AI SaaS industry include OpenAI, Google, IBM, and Microsoft.

5. Identifying a Problem to Solve: To build a successful generative AI SaaS startup, it is essential to identify a specific problem or need that your product can address.

6. Understanding the Target Market: Understanding your target market is critical to developing a product that meets their specific needs and preferences.

7. Building a Team: Building a skilled and diverse team is essential for success in the generative AI SaaS industry.

8. Creating a Business Plan: Creating a comprehensive business plan is critical for securing funding and charting a course for success.

9. Funding Options: There are several funding options available to generative AI SaaS startups, including venture capital, crowdfunding, and bootstrapping.
10. Developing the Product Roadmap: Developing a comprehensive product roadmap is essential for building a product that meets the needs of your target market.
11. Choosing the Right AI Technology: Choosing the right AI technology is essential for building a product that is both effective and scalable.
12. Designing the User Interface: Designing a user-friendly interface is critical for ensuring user engagement and satisfaction.
13. Ensuring Scalability and Performance: Ensuring that your product can scale to meet growing demand is essential for long-term success.
14. Identifying the Right Marketing Channels: Identifying the right marketing channels is critical for reaching your target market and driving user acquisition.
15. Developing a Pricing Strategy: Developing a pricing strategy that is both competitive and sustainable is critical for success in the generative AI SaaS industry.
16. Sales Tactics: Developing effective sales tactics is essential for driving user acquisition and revenue growth.
17. Establishing Customer Relationships: Building strong customer relationships is essential for ensuring user satisfaction and driving long-term revenue growth.
18. Expanding the Product Offering: Expanding your product offering to meet evolving user needs is critical for maintaining a competitive edge.
19. Scaling the Team: Scaling your team to meet growing demand is essential for ensuring long-term success.
20. Creating a Sustainable Business Model: Creating a sustainable business model is essential for achieving long-term profitability and growth.

21. Preparing for Acquisition or IPO: Preparing for acquisition or IPO is a critical step in achieving long-term success in the generative AI SaaS industry.
22. Data Privacy and Security Concerns: Ensuring data privacy and security is essential for maintaining user trust and compliance with regulatory requirements.
23. Ethical Considerations: Ethical considerations, such as bias and transparency, are critical for building trust with users and ensuring the responsible use of AI technology.
24. Competing with Established Players: Competing with established players in the generative AI SaaS industry requires a strong understanding of the competitive landscape.

- Generative AI refers to AI models that are capable of generating new and original data or content, such as images, text, or music.
- SaaS stands for software as a service, which is a business model where customers pay to access software over the internet.
- Generative AI SaaS is an emerging industry that offers a range of new and exciting opportunities for entrepreneurs and investors.
- To build a successful generative AI SaaS startup, it is important to identify a problem to solve, understand the target market, build a strong team, and create a solid business plan.
- Other key considerations include choosing the right AI technology, designing the user interface, ensuring scalability and performance, and developing a marketing and sales strategy.
- It is important to stay up-to-date with emerging trends in the industry, and to prioritize data privacy, security, and ethical considerations.

- Ultimately, the goal of a generative AI SaaS startup is to create a sustainable business model that can scale and grow over time, and potentially lead to acquisition or IPO.

Starting a generative AI SaaS startup can be a challenging but rewarding endeavor. By following the key points outlined in this book, entrepreneurs can set themselves up for success in this exciting and rapidly evolving industry.

Chapter 28: Future of Generative AI SaaS Startups

The future of generative AI SaaS startups is bright, with endless possibilities for innovation and growth. As the technology and tools for generative AI continue to evolve, we can expect to see a continued proliferation of startups in this space, and a growing demand for generative AI-powered solutions.

One key trend that is likely to shape the future of generative AI SaaS is the increasing availability of pre-trained models and tools. As more and more organizations and developers start to experiment with generative AI, there will be a growing need for off-the-shelf solutions that can be easily integrated into existing workflows and applications. This will create new opportunities for startups that specialize in building pre-trained models and tools for specific use cases or industries.

Another trend that is likely to shape the future of generative AI SaaS is the increasing importance of explainability and transparency. As generative AI is used in more sensitive and high-stakes applications, such as healthcare or finance, there will be a growing demand for solutions that can explain their decision-making and provide transparency into their inner workings. This will create new opportunities for startups that specialize in building explainable and transparent generative AI models.

Additionally, we can expect to see more and more startups leveraging the power of generative AI to create entirely new products and experiences. For example, we may see new startups emerge that specialize in using generative AI to create personalized fashion or home decor products, or to generate new forms of entertainment such as games or immersive virtual experiences.

Overall, the future of generative AI SaaS startups is bright, with new and exciting opportunities for innovation and growth. As the technology and tools for generative AI continue to evolve, we can expect to see a continued proliferation of startups in this space, and a growing demand for generative AI-powered solutions that can help organizations solve complex problems and create new and innovative products and experiences.

Chapter 29: Final Thoughts and Recommendations

As we've explored in this book, the world of generative AI SaaS startups is full of exciting possibilities and opportunities for innovation and growth. However, building a successful generative AI SaaS startup is not easy, and requires careful planning, execution, and a strong understanding of both the technology and the target market.

As you embark on your own journey to build a generative AI SaaS startup, there are a few key takeaways and recommendations to keep in mind:

1. Focus on solving a real problem: The most successful generative AI SaaS startups are those that are focused on solving a real problem for their target market. Spend time understanding the pain points and challenges facing your potential customers, and build your product and business model around addressing those needs.

2. Build a strong team: Building a successful generative AI SaaS startup requires a team with a diverse set of skills and expertise, including AI research, engineering, design, and business strategy. Make sure to bring on team members who share your vision and can contribute to building a strong and sustainable business.

3. Choose the right technology: There are many different AI technologies and tools available for building generative AI-powered solutions. Make sure to choose the technology that is best suited to your use case and target market, and be prepared to invest in ongoing research and development as the technology continues to evolve.

4. Prioritize data privacy and ethics: As generative AI becomes more pervasive and powerful, it is important to prioritize data privacy and ethical considerations in your product development and business practices. Build transparency and explainability into your models, and ensure that you are collecting and handling data in a responsible and ethical manner.
5. Be prepared to pivot and iterate: Building a successful generative AI SaaS startup requires a willingness to pivot and iterate based on feedback and changing market conditions. Be open to feedback from your customers and team members, and be prepared to adjust your product and business model accordingly.

As you navigate the complex and rapidly evolving world of generative AI SaaS startups, remember that building a successful business is a marathon, not a sprint. Focus on building a strong foundation, and be prepared to invest time, effort, and resources into growing and scaling your business over the long term. With a strong vision, a talented team, and a commitment to innovation and excellence, you can build a successful and sustainable generative AI SaaS startup that makes a real impact in the world.

I hope you have enjoyed this book and found it to be a valuable resource in your journey to start and grow a successful generative AI SaaS startup. My goal in writing this book was to provide you with practical advice and insights from industry professionals, as well as to inspire you to pursue your entrepreneurial dreams in the exciting field of AI and machine learning.

I wish you the best of luck in your endeavors, and I hope that this book has helped you to identify opportunities, overcome challenges, and achieve success in this rapidly evolving industry. Thank you for taking the time to read this book, and I hope it has been a valuable investment in your personal and professional growth.

# Epilogue: The Future of New Generative AI SaaS Startup

As the New Generative AI SaaS Startup continues to grow and evolve, it remains at the forefront of innovation in the field of artificial intelligence. Its cutting-edge technology has revolutionized the way businesses approach problem-solving, creativity, and decision-making.

Through its ongoing commitment to research and development, the New Generative AI SaaS Startup has continued to expand its capabilities and improve its offerings. Its advanced algorithms and machine learning models have helped businesses across industries to streamline their workflows, optimize their operations, and unlock new opportunities for growth.

But the New Generative AI SaaS Startup's impact extends far beyond the business world. Its technology has the potential to revolutionize fields such as healthcare, education, and environmental sustainability, unlocking new possibilities for human progress and social impact.

As the New Generative AI SaaS Startup looks towards the future, it remains committed to its core values of innovation, collaboration, and social responsibility. Its team of dedicated experts continues to push the boundaries of what's possible with AI, unlocking new potential for businesses and society as a whole.

With its focus on generative AI and its innovative approach to problem-solving, the New Generative AI SaaS Startup is poised to remain a key player in the rapidly evolving world of artificial intelligence for years to come. Its future is bright, and its potential is limitless.

www.ingramcontent.com/pod-product-compliance
Lightning Source LLC
LaVergne TN
LVHW051613050326
832903LV00033B/4478